Chapter 1: Introduction to Artificial Intelligence

What is Artificial Intelligence?

Artificial Intelligence, or AI, is a revolutionary technology that is transforming industries and creating endless possibilities for innovation. At its core, AI refers to the simulation of human intelligence processes by machines, including learning, reasoning, problem-solving, and decision-making. It is truly the future of technology, and as a founder looking to create an AI startup, understanding what AI is and how it can benefit your business is crucial.

AI has the power to automate tasks, improve efficiency, and make data-driven decisions like never before. By leveraging AI technology, startups can streamline operations, personalize customer experiences, and gain valuable insights from data. The potential for growth and success with AI is limitless, and as a founder, it is essential to embrace this technology and incorporate it into your business strategy.

One of the key components of AI is machine learning, which allows machines to learn from data and improve their performance over time without being explicitly programmed. This capability enables AI systems to adapt to new information, make predictions, and solve complex problems. By harnessing the power of machine learning, startups can create intelligent products and services that meet the needs of their customers in real-time.

Another important aspect of AI is natural language processing, which enables machines to understand, interpret, and generate human language. This technology is revolutionizing the way we communicate with machines, allowing for more seamless interactions and personalized experiences. By integrating natural language processing into your AI startup, you can create chatbots, virtual assistants, and other applications that enhance customer engagement and satisfaction.

In conclusion, understanding what AI is and how it can benefit your startup is essential for success in today's tech-driven world. By embracing AI technology, founders can unlock new opportunities, drive innovation, and create value for their customers. As you embark on your journey to create an AI startup, remember that the possibilities are endless with AI – all it takes is vision, determination, and a willingness to embrace the future of technology.

The Importance of AI in Tech Startups

AI technology has become a game-changer in the world of tech startups, revolutionizing the way businesses operate and innovate. As a founder looking to create an AI startup, understanding the importance of AI in your venture is crucial to staying ahead of the curve and making a lasting impact in the industry. AI has the power to transform your business model, streamline processes, improve decision-making, and enhance customer experiences like never before.

One of the key reasons why AI is so important for tech startups is its ability to drive innovation and competitiveness. By leveraging AI technology, startups can develop unique products and services that stand out in the market and attract a loyal customer base. AI empowers founders to think outside the box, experiment with new ideas, and create solutions that address pressing challenges in innovative ways. With AI, the possibilities are endless, and the potential for success is limitless.

Furthermore, AI plays a crucial role in improving operational efficiency and scalability for tech startups. By automating repetitive tasks, analyzing vast amounts of data, and optimizing workflows, AI can help startups save time, reduce costs, and increase productivity. This allows founders to focus on strategic decision-making, growth opportunities, and building a strong foundation for their startup to thrive in the long run.

In addition, AI enables tech startups to make data-driven decisions that are based on real-time insights and predictive analytics. By harnessing the power of AI algorithms, startups can uncover valuable patterns, trends, and correlations in their data that can inform strategic planning, marketing strategies, and product development. This data-driven approach not only leads to smarter decision-making but also helps startups stay agile and responsive to changing market dynamics.

In conclusion, the importance of AI in tech startups cannot be overstated. As a founder looking to create an AI startup, embracing AI technology is not just a competitive advantage but a necessity for staying relevant and innovative in today's fast-paced digital landscape. By harnessing the power of AI to drive innovation, improve operational efficiency, and make data-driven decisions, founders can pave the way for a successful and sustainable startup that has the potential to make a lasting impact on the industry.

Overview of Building a Tech Startup

Welcome to the exciting world of building a tech startup focused on artificial intelligence (AI)! In this subchapter, we will provide you with an overview of the key steps involved in creating a successful AI startup. As a Founder in the niche of AI, you have the opportunity to harness the power of cutting-edge technology to solve complex problems and disrupt traditional industries. By following the guidelines outlined in this chapter, you will be well on your way to building a successful tech startup from scratch.

The first step in building a tech startup is to identify a problem or opportunity that can be addressed using AI technology. This could be anything from improving customer service through chatbots to optimizing supply chain logistics using machine learning algorithms. By focusing on a specific problem or niche, you can differentiate your startup from competitors and attract customers who are looking for innovative solutions.

Once you have identified a problem or opportunity, the next step is to develop a minimum viable product (MVP) that demonstrates the value of your AI solution. This could be a prototype of your AI software or a proof-of-concept that shows how your technology can solve the identified problem. By creating an MVP, you can test your assumptions, gather feedback from potential customers, and iterate on your product to ensure it meets market needs.

After developing your MVP, the next step is to build a team of talented individuals who can help bring your vision to life. This may include hiring data scientists, software engineers, and business development professionals who have experience working with AI technology. By assembling a diverse team with complementary skills, you can ensure that your startup has the expertise needed to succeed in the competitive AI market.

As you work towards launching your AI startup, it is important to focus on building a strong brand and establishing a presence in the market. This could involve creating a compelling website, engaging in social media marketing, and attending industry conferences and events to network with potential customers and investors. By building awareness and credibility for your startup, you can attract the attention of key stakeholders and secure the resources needed to scale your business and achieve long-term success. Remember, building a tech startup is a challenging but rewarding journey that requires perseverance, passion, and a willingness to take risks. By following the steps outlined in this subchapter and staying true to your vision, you can create a successful AI startup that makes a positive impact on the world.

Chapter 2: Understanding the Market

Market Research for AI Startups

Market research is a crucial step for any startup, especially for those in the AI industry. As a founder looking to build a successful AI startup from scratch, conducting comprehensive market research is key to understanding the landscape and identifying opportunities for growth. By gaining insights into the market, you can make informed decisions that will drive the success of your AI startup.

When conducting market research for your AI startup, it's important to start by identifying your target audience. Who are the potential customers for your AI product or service? What are their pain points and needs that your AI solution can address? By understanding your target audience, you can tailor your product to meet their specific needs and stand out in the competitive AI market.

In addition to understanding your target audience, it's essential to analyze the competition in the AI industry. Who are your competitors, and what are their strengths and weaknesses? By conducting a thorough competitive analysis, you can identify gaps in the market and position your AI startup as a unique and innovative player in the industry. This will help you differentiate your product and attract customers who are looking for a fresh approach to AI solutions.

Furthermore, market research can also help you identify trends and opportunities in the AI industry. By staying informed about the latest developments in AI technology and applications, you can position your startup to take advantage of emerging trends and capitalize on new opportunities. This proactive approach to market research will help you stay ahead of the curve and position your AI startup for long-term success.

In conclusion, market research is a critical component of building a successful AI startup from scratch. By understanding your target audience, analyzing the competition, and identifying trends and opportunities in the AI industry, you can make informed decisions that will drive the growth and success of your startup. So, as a founder looking to create an AI startup, remember to prioritize market research and use it as a guiding tool to build a thriving business in the ever-evolving AI landscape.

Identifying Your Target Audience

Identifying Your Target Audience is crucial for the success of your AI startup. As a Founder, understanding who your ideal customers are is the first step towards building a successful business. By knowing your target audience, you can tailor your product or service to meet their needs and preferences, increasing the chances of gaining loyal customers.

Start by conducting market research to identify the demographics, interests, and pain points of your target audience. This will help you create a customer profile that outlines who your ideal customers are and what motivates them to purchase your product. By understanding your target audience on a deeper level, you can better position your AI startup to attract and retain customers.

Once you have identified your target audience, it's important to tailor your marketing strategies to reach them effectively. This may include creating targeted advertising campaigns, optimizing your website for search engines, and leveraging social media platforms to engage with your target audience. By focusing your efforts on reaching the right people, you can maximize the impact of your marketing efforts and drive more traffic to your AI startup.

In addition to marketing strategies, it's important to listen to feedback from your target audience to continuously improve your product or service. By soliciting feedback through surveys, focus groups, or customer reviews, you can gain valuable insights into what your customers like and dislike about your AI startup. Use this feedback to make adjustments and enhancements that align with the preferences of your target audience, ultimately leading to increased customer satisfaction and loyalty.

In conclusion, identifying your target audience is a critical step in building a successful AI startup. By understanding who your ideal customers are, tailoring your marketing strategies to reach them effectively, and listening to their feedback to improve your product or service, you can position your startup for long-term success. Remember, your target audience is the key to unlocking the full potential of your AI startup, so make it a priority to identify and engage with them from the very beginning.

Analyzing Competitors in the AI Industry

As a Founder looking to create a successful AI startup, one of the most crucial aspects of your business strategy should be analyzing your competitors in the AI industry. By understanding who your competitors are, what they offer, and how they position themselves in the market, you can gain valuable insights that will help you differentiate your own startup and stand out from the crowd.

When analyzing your competitors in the AI industry, it's important to look beyond just their products and services. Take the time to research their target audience, their marketing strategies, and their overall brand positioning. By understanding how your competitors are reaching and engaging with their customers, you can identify areas where you can improve and develop your own unique approach to building your startup.

Another key aspect of analyzing your competitors in the AI industry is studying their strengths and weaknesses. By identifying what your competitors do well and where they may be falling short, you can capitalize on opportunities to outperform them in the market. Use this information to refine your own business strategy and focus on areas where you can offer a superior product or service to your target audience.

Furthermore, don't be afraid to learn from your competitors in the AI industry. Take note of what they are doing right and how they are effectively engaging with their customers. Use this knowledge to inspire your own innovative ideas and push the boundaries of what is possible in the AI industry. By staying informed and open to new insights, you can position your startup for success and set yourself apart from the competition.

In conclusion, analyzing your competitors in the AI industry is a vital step in building a successful startup from scratch. By studying their strategies, strengths, and weaknesses, you can gain valuable insights that will help you differentiate your business and attract customers. Use this information to inspire your own innovative ideas and push the boundaries of what is possible in the AI industry. Stay informed, stay inspired, and stay ahead of the competition as you embark on your journey to create a thriving AI startup.

Chapter 3: Developing Your AI Idea

Brainstorming AI Solutions

As a founder looking to create an AI startup, one of the most crucial steps in the journey is brainstorming AI solutions. This process involves tapping into the creative potential of your team and exploring innovative ways to address problems using artificial intelligence technology. By engaging in brainstorming sessions, you not only generate new ideas but also foster collaboration and teamwork within your startup.

When brainstorming AI solutions, it is important to think outside the box and challenge conventional thinking. Encourage your team to explore different angles and perspectives, and to consider how AI can be applied in unique and transformative ways. By pushing boundaries and embracing a spirit of curiosity, you open the door to groundbreaking innovations that can set your startup apart in the competitive AI landscape.

One effective strategy for brainstorming AI solutions is to conduct research and stay informed about the latest developments in the field. By keeping abreast of industry trends and emerging technologies, you can gain valuable insights that can inspire new ideas and approaches. Additionally, networking with other AI professionals and attending industry events can provide opportunities for collaboration and knowledge sharing, further fueling the brainstorming process.

Another key aspect of brainstorming AI solutions is to prioritize problem-solving and addressing real-world challenges. Consider the pain points and needs of your target audience, and focus on developing solutions that offer tangible benefits and value. By aligning your AI startup with a clear mission and purpose, you can create meaningful solutions that resonate with customers and drive success.

In conclusion, brainstorming AI solutions is a dynamic and collaborative process that is essential for the success of your AI startup. By fostering a culture of creativity, innovation, and problem-solving, you can unlock the full potential of artificial intelligence technology and create groundbreaking solutions that have a lasting impact. Embrace the power of brainstorming and unleash the full potential of your team to build a successful AI startup from scratch.

Validating Your AI Idea

As a founder looking to create an AI startup, it is crucial to validate your AI idea before diving into the development process. Validating your idea will not only save you time and resources but will also ensure that you are solving a real problem for your target audience. In this subchapter, we will explore the importance of validating your AI idea and provide you with practical tips on how to do so effectively.

The first step in validating your AI idea is to conduct market research. This involves identifying your target audience, understanding their pain points, and assessing the competition in the market. By conducting thorough market research, you can gain valuable insights into the demand for your AI solution and identify any gaps in the market that your idea can fill.

In addition to market research, it is essential to gather feedback from potential users and stakeholders. This can be done through surveys, interviews, or focus groups. By engaging with your target audience early on, you can gain valuable feedback on your AI idea, identify any potential issues or limitations, and make necessary adjustments before moving forward.

Another important aspect of validating your AI idea is to build a minimum viable product (MVP). An MVP is a simplified version of your AI solution that allows you to test the core functionality and gather feedback from users. By building an MVP, you can quickly iterate on your idea, validate its feasibility, and make informed decisions on whether to proceed with further development.

In conclusion, validating your AI idea is a crucial step in the process of building a successful AI startup. By conducting market research, gathering feedback from users, and building an MVP, you can ensure that your AI idea is solving a real problem for your target audience and has the potential for success. Remember, validation is key to building a sustainable and scalable AI startup from scratch.

Creating a Unique Value Proposition

Creating a unique value proposition is crucial for any startup, but it is especially important when it comes to building an AI startup. With the rapidly evolving landscape of artificial intelligence, it is more important than ever to stand out from the competition and offer something truly innovative to your customers. In this chapter, we will explore how you can create a unique value proposition that sets your AI startup apart from the rest.

The first step in creating a unique value proposition for your AI startup is to identify your target market and understand their needs and pain points. By conducting thorough market research and gathering feedback from potential customers, you can gain valuable insights into what sets your target market apart and how you can address their specific needs with your AI technology. This will enable you to tailor your value proposition to meet the unique challenges and opportunities of your target market.

Once you have a clear understanding of your target market, it is important to define what sets your AI startup apart from the competition. This could be a unique technology or algorithm that you have developed, a specialized industry focus, or a different approach to solving a common problem. Whatever it is, make sure that your unique value proposition is clear, concise, and easy to understand. This will help you communicate the value of your AI startup to potential customers and investors.

In addition to defining your unique value proposition, it is important to communicate it effectively to your target market. This means developing a strong brand identity that reflects your values and mission, as well as creating compelling marketing materials that clearly communicate the benefits of your AI technology. By effectively communicating your unique value proposition, you can attract the right customers and investors who share your vision and believe in the potential of your AI startup.

Creating a unique value proposition for your AI startup is not easy, but with the right approach and mindset, you can set your company apart from the competition and position yourself for success in the rapidly evolving world of artificial intelligence. By identifying your target market, defining what sets your AI startup apart, and effectively communicating your value proposition, you can build a strong foundation for your company and attract the right customers and investors who believe in your vision. Remember, the key to success in the AI startup world is to be innovative, bold, and always focused on delivering value to your customers.

Chapter 4: Building Your AI Team

Hiring AI Experts

Hiring AI experts is crucial for the success of any AI startup. These individuals possess the specialized skills and knowledge necessary to develop cutting-edge artificial intelligence technologies that can propel your company to the next level. When it comes to building a tech startup from scratch, having a team of talented AI experts is essential.

One of the first steps in hiring AI experts is to clearly define the roles and responsibilities that you need them to fulfill within your company. Whether you are looking for data scientists, machine learning engineers, or AI researchers, having a clear understanding of the specific skills and expertise required for each position will help you attract the right candidates.

When it comes to recruiting AI experts, it is important to cast a wide net and explore various channels for finding top talent. This may include attending industry conferences, networking events, and reaching out to universities and research institutions where AI experts are likely to be found. Additionally, leveraging online job boards and professional networking sites can help you connect with potential candidates who possess the skills and experience you are looking for.

Once you have identified potential candidates, it is important to conduct thorough interviews to assess their technical capabilities, problem-solving skills, and cultural fit within your company. Look for candidates who not only have a strong technical background in artificial intelligence but also demonstrate a passion for innovation and a willingness to collaborate with others to achieve common goals.

In conclusion, hiring AI experts is a critical step in building a successful AI startup. By attracting top talent with the right skills and expertise, you can create a dynamic team that is capable of developing groundbreaking AI technologies that will drive your company's growth and success. Remember to define clear roles and responsibilities, cast a wide net in your search for talent, and conduct thorough interviews to ensure that you are hiring the best AI experts for your company.

Building a Diverse and Inclusive Team

Building a diverse and inclusive team is crucial for the success of any AI startup. As a founder, it is your responsibility to create a work environment where everyone feels welcome and valued for their unique perspectives and experiences. By fostering diversity and inclusion within your team, you are not only creating a more innovative and creative work environment, but you are also setting your startup up for long-term success.

One of the key benefits of building a diverse team is the ability to tap into a wide range of perspectives and ideas. When you have team members from different backgrounds, cultures, and experiences, you are able to approach problems from a variety of angles and come up with more creative solutions. This diversity of thought can give your AI startup a competitive edge in the rapidly evolving tech industry.

In addition to fostering creativity and innovation, building a diverse and inclusive team can also help your startup attract top talent. In today's competitive job market, top candidates are looking for companies that value diversity and inclusion. By creating a work environment where everyone feels welcome and respected, you are more likely to attract and retain top talent in the AI industry.

Furthermore, a diverse and inclusive team can also lead to better decision-making and problem-solving. Studies have shown that diverse teams are more effective at solving complex problems and making sound decisions. By creating a team that is made up of individuals with different backgrounds and perspectives, you are better equipped to tackle the challenges that come with building and growing an AI startup.

In conclusion, building a diverse and inclusive team is not only the right thing to do, but it is also essential for the success of your AI startup. By creating a work environment where everyone feels valued and respected, you are fostering creativity, innovation, and better decision-making within your team. As a founder, it is important to prioritize diversity and inclusion in order to set your startup up for long-term success in the competitive tech industry.

Fostering a Collaborative Team Culture

Fostering a collaborative team culture is essential for the success of any AI startup. As a founder, it is your responsibility to create an environment where team members feel empowered to share their ideas, collaborate with one another, and work towards a common goal. By fostering a collaborative team culture, you can harness the collective intelligence and creativity of your team to drive innovation and achieve your startup's objectives.

One of the key ways to foster a collaborative team culture is to lead by example. As the founder of the AI startup, it is important that you demonstrate a willingness to listen to your team members, value their input, and work together to solve problems. By showing that you are open to collaboration and willing to work as a team, you can inspire your team members to do the same.

Another important aspect of fostering a collaborative team culture is to create opportunities for team members to work together on projects and initiatives. By assigning tasks that require collaboration and teamwork, you can help your team members build strong relationships, trust one another, and communicate effectively. Encouraging open communication and collaboration can lead to greater efficiency, creativity, and overall success for your AI startup.

In addition to leading by example and creating opportunities for collaboration, it is also important to establish clear goals and expectations for your team. By setting clear objectives and defining roles and responsibilities, you can help your team members understand what is expected of them and how their work contributes to the success of the startup. Providing regular feedback and recognition for team members' contributions can also help to foster a collaborative team culture and motivate team members to work together towards a common goal.

In conclusion, fostering a collaborative team culture is essential for the success of your AI startup. By leading by example, creating opportunities for collaboration, and setting clear goals and expectations, you can inspire your team members to work together towards a common goal. By harnessing the collective intelligence and creativity of your team, you can drive innovation, achieve your startup's objectives, and create a culture of collaboration that will set your AI startup up for success.

Chapter 5: Creating a Business Plan

Defining Your AI Startup's Mission and Vision

As a founder looking to create an AI startup, it is crucial to clearly define your mission and vision for your company. Your mission is the reason your company exists, the driving force behind all that you do. It is what sets you apart from your competitors and guides your decision-making process. Your vision is the ultimate goal you aspire to achieve, the future you are working towards. It is what inspires and motivates you and your team to keep pushing forward, even in the face of challenges.

When defining your AI startup's mission, think about the impact you want to have on the world. How do you want to use artificial intelligence to solve real-world problems and improve people's lives? Your mission should be bold and aspirational, reflecting your passion and commitment to making a difference. It should be something that resonates with you and your team on a deep level, driving you to work harder and push boundaries.

Your vision for your AI startup should be equally inspiring. What do you ultimately want to achieve with your company? How do you see artificial intelligence transforming industries and shaping the future? Your vision should be ambitious and forward-thinking, painting a picture of the world you want to create with your technology. It should be a beacon of hope and inspiration, guiding you and your team towards a common goal.

By clearly defining your AI startup's mission and vision, you set the foundation for everything you do as a founder. Your mission will guide your strategic decisions, helping you stay focused on what truly matters. Your vision will inspire and motivate you and your team, pushing you to achieve great things. Together, your mission and vision will shape the identity of your company, attracting like-minded individuals who share your passion and values.

In the fast-paced world of AI startups, having a clear mission and vision is essential for success. It gives you a sense of purpose and direction, helping you navigate the challenges and uncertainties of entrepreneurship. So take the time to define your AI startup's mission and vision with care and thoughtfulness. Let them be the guiding lights that lead you towards building a tech startup that not only makes a profit but also makes a difference in the world.

Setting SMART Goals for Your AI Startup

Setting SMART goals for your AI startup is crucial to ensuring that your business stays on track and continues to grow and thrive. SMART goals are Specific, Measurable, Achievable, Relevant, and Time-bound. By setting these types of goals for your startup, you can create a roadmap for success and ensure that you are constantly moving towards your ultimate vision.

When setting goals for your AI startup, it's important to be specific about what you want to achieve. Instead of setting a vague goal like "increase revenue," try setting a specific goal like "increase revenue by 20% in the next quarter." This gives you a clear target to aim for and helps keep you focused on what needs to be done to achieve it.

Measurable goals are essential for tracking your progress and determining whether or not you are on track to meet your objectives. By setting measurable goals, you can easily track your progress and make adjustments as needed to stay on course. This will help you stay accountable and ensure that you are constantly working towards your goals.

Achievable goals are ones that are realistic and attainable given the resources and constraints of your AI startup. It's important to set goals that stretch you and push you out of your comfort zone, but they should also be achievable with hard work and dedication. By setting achievable goals, you can build momentum and confidence as you see yourself making progress towards your ultimate vision.

Relevant goals are ones that are aligned with the overall vision and mission of your AI startup. It's important to set goals that are relevant to your business and that will help you move closer to achieving your long-term objectives. By setting relevant goals, you can ensure that you are always moving in the right direction and that your efforts are focused on what truly matters for the success of your startup.

Finally, time-bound goals are ones that have a specific deadline attached to them. By setting time-bound goals, you create a sense of urgency and momentum that can help drive you towards success. Setting deadlines for your goals also helps you prioritize your tasks and manage your time effectively, ensuring that you are always working towards your objectives in a timely manner.

In conclusion, setting SMART goals for your AI startup is essential for guiding your business towards success. By being specific, measurable, achievable, relevant, and time-bound in your goal-setting process, you can create a clear roadmap for your startup and ensure that you are constantly moving in the right direction. So, take the time to set SMART goals for your AI startup today and watch as your business grows and thrives as a result.

Financial Planning for Your AI Startup

As a Founder looking to create an AI startup, one of the most crucial aspects of your business plan should be financial planning. Building a sustainable financial foundation for your AI startup will not only ensure its success but also pave the way for future growth and innovation. In this subchapter, we will delve into the key components of financial planning for your AI startup, offering insights and strategies to help you navigate the financial landscape with confidence and clarity.

The first step in financial planning for your AI startup is to establish a clear understanding of your business model and revenue streams. Identify your target market, assess the competitive landscape, and determine how your AI technology will add value to your customers. By aligning your financial goals with your business objectives, you can develop a roadmap for sustainable growth and profitability.

Once you have a solid understanding of your business model, it's time to create a detailed financial forecast for your AI startup. This forecast should include projected revenues, expenses, and cash flow projections for the next 1-3 years. By forecasting your financial performance, you can identify potential risks and opportunities, make informed decisions, and stay on track towards achieving your financial goals.

In addition to creating a financial forecast, it's important to establish a budget and monitor your financial performance on a regular basis. Keep track of your cash flow, expenses, and revenues, and make adjustments as needed to ensure that your AI startup remains on a solid financial footing. By maintaining financial discipline and transparency, you can build trust with investors and stakeholders, and position your AI startup for long-term success.

In conclusion, financial planning is a critical component of building a successful AI startup. By taking a strategic approach to financial planning, you can set your AI startup up for success, secure funding, and achieve your business goals. Stay focused, stay diligent, and remember that financial planning is not just about numbers — it's about creating a solid foundation for your AI startup to thrive and make a lasting impact in the world.

Chapter 6: Funding Your AI Startup

Bootstrapping vs. Raising Venture Capital

As a founder looking to create an AI startup, one of the biggest decisions you'll face is whether to bootstrap your way to success or seek venture capital funding. Both paths have their own set of advantages and challenges, and it's crucial to understand the implications of each before making a decision.

Bootstrapping, or self-funding your startup, can be a great way to maintain full control over your company and its direction. By relying on your own resources and revenue, you can avoid the pressures and expectations that come with external funding. This can give you the freedom to build your product at your own pace and prioritize what truly matters for your vision.

On the other hand, raising venture capital can provide the financial resources and expertise needed to scale your AI startup quickly. With the right investors on board, you can access valuable industry connections, guidance, and support that can help accelerate your growth. Venture capital can also help you stay ahead of the competition and take advantage of emerging opportunities in the market.

However, it's important to remember that venture capital comes with its own set of challenges. Investors will expect a return on their investment, which can put pressure on you to deliver results quickly. You may also have to give up a portion of ownership and control of your company, which can impact your decision-making autonomy.

Ultimately, the decision to bootstrap or raise venture capital will depend on your individual goals, resources, and risk tolerance. Whichever path you choose, remember that building a successful AI startup requires hard work, dedication, and a clear vision. Trust in your abilities as a founder and stay focused on creating a product that truly solves a problem for your target audience. With the right mindset and strategy, you can build a thriving AI startup that makes a meaningful impact in the world.

Pitching Your AI Startup to Investors

As a founder in the competitive world of AI startups, one of the most crucial steps in building your tech company from scratch is pitching your idea to potential investors. This is your chance to showcase the innovation and potential of your AI startup, and convince investors to believe in your vision. Remember, you are not just selling a product or service - you are selling the future of technology.

When pitching your AI startup to investors, it is essential to clearly communicate your value proposition. What problem does your AI solution solve? How is it different from existing technologies? What sets your startup apart from the competition? Be concise and compelling in your pitch, and make sure to highlight the unique advantages of your AI technology.

In addition to clearly articulating your value proposition, it is important to demonstrate the market potential of your AI startup. Investors want to see that there is a demand for your product or service, and that you have a clear strategy for capturing market share. Present market research, customer testimonials, and financial projections to support your claims and show investors that your AI startup has the potential for significant growth.

Another key aspect of pitching your AI startup to investors is showcasing your team's expertise and track record. Investors want to know that you have the right team in place to execute on your vision and drive the success of your startup. Highlight the skills and experience of your team members, and demonstrate how their collective strengths will help your AI startup succeed in the competitive tech industry.

Finally, when pitching your AI startup to investors, it is important to convey your passion and commitment to your vision. Investors want to see that you believe in your product and are willing to put in the hard work to make it a success. Show your determination, resilience, and entrepreneurial spirit, and inspire investors to join you on your journey to revolutionize the world of AI technology. Remember, with the right pitch and the right mindset, you can attract the funding you need to turn your AI startup into a thriving tech company.

Securing Funding for Your AI Startup

Securing funding for your AI startup is a crucial step in turning your vision into reality. As a founder, you must be prepared to articulate your unique value proposition and convince investors of the potential for success. Remember, funding is not just about money - it's about finding partners who believe in your mission and are willing to support you on your journey.

One of the first things you'll need to do is create a solid business plan that outlines your goals, target market, competition, and financial projections. This will not only help you clarify your vision but also demonstrate to potential investors that you have a clear path to success. Be sure to highlight the unique ways in which your AI technology sets you apart from the competition and how it can solve real-world problems.

When seeking funding for your AI startup, it's important to cast a wide net and explore all possible avenues. This could include pitching to venture capitalists, angel investors, accelerators, or even crowdfunding platforms. Each of these sources of funding has its own set of pros and cons, so be sure to do your research and tailor your pitch accordingly.

Building relationships with potential investors is key to securing funding for your AI startup. Take the time to network at industry events, conferences, and pitch competitions. Be prepared to share your story and passion for your technology, and don't be afraid to ask for advice or feedback. Investors want to see that you are committed and willing to do whatever it takes to make your startup successful.

Above all, remember that securing funding for your AI startup is a journey, not a destination. Stay resilient in the face of rejection and continue to refine your pitch and business plan based on feedback. With perseverance, passion, and a clear vision, you can attract the right investors who will help you bring your AI startup to life.

Chapter 7: Developing Your Minimum Viable Product (MVP)

Designing Your AI Product

Congratulations on taking the first step towards building your AI startup! As a Founder embarking on this exciting journey, it's crucial to understand the importance of designing your AI product. The design phase is where your vision comes to life, where you shape the future of your company and create a product that will revolutionize the industry.

When designing your AI product, it's essential to start with a clear understanding of your target audience and their needs. Conduct thorough market research to identify pain points and challenges that your product can solve. By understanding your audience, you can tailor your AI product to meet their specific requirements and ensure its success in the market.

Next, focus on defining the key features and functionalities of your AI product. What sets your product apart from competitors? What value does it bring to users? By clearly outlining these aspects, you can create a unique selling proposition that will attract customers and differentiate your product in a crowded market.

In the design phase, it's also important to consider the user experience (UX) of your AI product. A seamless and intuitive user interface can make a significant difference in how your product is perceived and adopted by users. By prioritizing UX design, you can enhance user satisfaction, increase retention rates, and drive customer loyalty.

Lastly, don't forget to test and iterate on your AI product design. Gather feedback from early adopters, conduct usability tests, and make improvements based on user input. Embrace a culture of continuous improvement and innovation to ensure that your AI product evolves with the changing needs of your customers. Remember, designing your AI product is a dynamic process that requires creativity, flexibility, and a deep understanding of your market. By following these guidelines, you can create a cutting-edge AI product that will propel your startup to success.

Testing and Iterating Your AI MVP

Congratulations, Founder! You have successfully created your AI Minimum Viable Product (MVP). Now comes the crucial stage of testing and iterating to ensure that your AI solution is ready to meet the needs of your target audience. This phase is where you will gather valuable feedback, make necessary improvements, and ultimately refine your product to perfection.

Testing your AI MVP is not just about fixing bugs or technical issues. It is about understanding how your target users interact with your product, what features they find most valuable, and what improvements can be made to enhance their experience. By conducting thorough testing and gathering feedback from real users, you will gain valuable insights that will guide your product development process.

Iterating on your AI MVP is a continuous process that involves making incremental improvements based on the feedback you receive. It is important to prioritize the most critical issues and focus on solving them first before moving on to other features or functionalities. By taking a systematic approach to iterating, you can ensure that your product evolves in a way that aligns with the needs and preferences of your target audience.

Remember, testing and iterating your AI MVP is not a one-time task but an ongoing process that will continue throughout the lifecycle of your product. Embrace each iteration as an opportunity to learn, grow, and improve your AI solution. By being open to feedback, staying agile, and remaining committed to delivering value to your users, you will set your AI startup on the path to success.

In conclusion, testing and iterating your AI MVP is a vital step in the journey of building a successful tech startup. By focusing on gathering user feedback, making incremental improvements, and continuously refining your product, you will create an AI solution that truly meets the needs of your target audience. Stay inspired, stay focused, and trust in the process as you work towards bringing your vision to life.

Launching Your AI MVP to the Market

Congratulations, Founder! You have successfully developed your AI Minimum Viable Product (MVP) and now it's time to launch it to the market. This is a crucial step in the journey of building your AI startup, and it's important to approach it with confidence and determination.

Before you launch your AI MVP to the market, it's essential to have a clear understanding of your target audience and their needs. Take the time to conduct market research and gather feedback from potential customers to ensure that your product is meeting their expectations. This will help you tailor your marketing strategy and messaging to resonate with your target audience.

Once you have a solid understanding of your target market, it's time to create a strong marketing plan to launch your AI MVP successfully. This plan should include a mix of online and offline marketing tactics, such as social media advertising, email campaigns, and partnerships with influencers in your industry. Remember, the key to a successful product launch is to create buzz and excitement around your AI MVP.

As you prepare to launch your AI MVP to the market, it's important to have a solid go-to-market strategy in place. This strategy should outline the steps you will take to introduce your product to your target audience, generate interest and drive sales. Be prepared to pivot and make adjustments to your strategy based on feedback from customers and market trends.

Launching your AI MVP to the market is an exciting and challenging process, but with the right mindset and strategy, you can set yourself up for success. Remember to stay focused on your goals, listen to feedback from customers, and be open to making changes as needed. With perseverance and determination, you can take your AI startup to new heights and make a significant impact in the tech industry.

Chapter 8: Scaling Your AI Startup

Growing Your Customer Base

As a Founder in the niche of creating an AI startup, one of the most crucial aspects of building a successful tech company is growing your customer base. Without a steady stream of customers, your business will struggle to thrive and reach its full potential. In this subchapter, we will explore some key strategies for expanding your customer base and attracting new clients to your AI startup.

The first step in growing your customer base is to clearly define your target market. Who are the individuals or companies that are most likely to benefit from your AI products or services? By understanding the needs and preferences of your target market, you can tailor your marketing efforts to attract the right customers. Conduct market research, gather data, and create detailed customer personas to guide your marketing strategy.

Once you have identified your target market, it's time to develop a strong marketing plan to reach potential customers. Utilize a combination of digital marketing, social media, content marketing, and traditional advertising to raise awareness about your AI startup and attract new customers. Consider partnering with influencers, attending industry events, and networking with other tech companies to expand your reach and connect with potential clients.

In addition to marketing efforts, building strong relationships with your existing customers is essential for growing your customer base. Happy customers are more likely to refer your AI startup to others and become repeat buyers. Provide exceptional customer service, gather feedback, and continually improve your products or services to ensure customer satisfaction and loyalty. By focusing on customer retention, you can create a loyal customer base that will help your AI startup thrive in the long run.

Another key strategy for growing your customer base is to leverage the power of referrals and word-of-mouth marketing. Encourage satisfied customers to spread the word about your AI startup to their networks and offer incentives for successful referrals. By harnessing the power of word-of-mouth marketing, you can quickly expand your customer base and attract new clients who are already primed to trust your brand. Remember, happy customers are your best advocates for growing your AI startup and attracting new business opportunities.

In conclusion, growing your customer base is a crucial aspect of building a successful AI startup. By defining your target market, developing a strong marketing plan, building strong relationships with customers, and leveraging the power of referrals, you can attract new clients and expand your business. Stay focused, stay dedicated, and always strive to exceed the expectations of your customers. With the right strategies and a customer-centric approach, you can grow your AI startup and achieve long-term success in the competitive tech industry.

Expanding Your AI Product Line

Congratulations! You have successfully launched your AI startup and have a product that is gaining traction in the market. Now it's time to think about expanding your AI product line to reach even greater heights of success. By diversifying your offerings, you can tap into new markets, attract more customers, and solidify your position as a leader in the AI industry.

One way to expand your AI product line is to identify new use cases for your existing technology. Take a close look at your current product and think about how it could be adapted or repurposed to solve different problems or meet the needs of different industries. By thinking creatively and being open to new possibilities, you can uncover new opportunities for growth and innovation.

Another strategy for expanding your AI product line is to explore partnerships and collaborations with other companies in the tech industry. By teaming up with complementary businesses, you can combine your expertise and resources to create new and exciting products that offer even greater value to customers. Collaborations can also help you reach new audiences and open up new avenues for distribution and sales.

In addition to exploring new use cases and forming partnerships, you may also want to consider developing new products from scratch that complement your existing offerings. Brainstorm ideas for new AI products that build on your core competencies and leverage your unique strengths. By expanding your product line in this way, you can diversify your revenue streams and stay ahead of the competition in a rapidly evolving market.

Expanding your AI product line is an exciting opportunity to take your startup to the next level and achieve even greater success. By thinking creatively, collaborating with others, and developing new products that complement your existing offerings, you can unlock new growth opportunities and solidify your position as a leader in the AI industry. Embrace the challenge of expanding your product line, and watch as your startup reaches new heights of innovation and profitability.

Scaling Your AI Infrastructure

As a Founder looking to create an AI startup, one of the most crucial aspects to consider is how to scale your AI infrastructure effectively. Scaling your AI infrastructure involves expanding your technology capabilities to meet the growing demands of your business and customers. This subchapter will provide you with valuable insights and strategies on how to scale your AI infrastructure successfully.

The first step in scaling your AI infrastructure is to assess your current technology stack and identify any bottlenecks or limitations that may hinder scalability. It is essential to have a solid foundation in place before scaling up. This may involve upgrading your hardware, optimizing your algorithms, or investing in cloud computing resources to handle increased data processing requirements.

Next, it is important to prioritize automation and efficiency in your AI infrastructure. By automating routine tasks and optimizing processes, you can free up resources to focus on more strategic initiatives that drive growth and innovation. Implementing tools and technologies such as machine learning algorithms and data pipelines can help streamline operations and improve the overall efficiency of your AI infrastructure.

Another key aspect of scaling your AI infrastructure is to build a scalable data architecture that can support the increasing volume and complexity of data generated by your AI systems. This may involve implementing data lakes, data warehouses, and data pipelines to ensure seamless data integration and processing. By designing a scalable data architecture, you can future-proof your AI infrastructure and enable it to adapt to changing business requirements.

In conclusion, scaling your AI infrastructure is a critical step in the growth and success of your AI startup. By assessing your current technology stack, prioritizing automation and efficiency, and building a scalable data architecture, you can position your AI startup for long-term success and sustainability. Remember, scalability is not just about expanding your technology capabilities but also about creating a solid foundation that can support your growth and innovation efforts.

Chapter 9: Building a Strong Brand

Defining Your AI Startup's Brand Identity

Defining Your AI Startup's Brand Identity is a crucial step in building a successful tech company from scratch. As a Founder in the AI startup niche, your brand identity is what sets you apart from the competition and attracts customers to your product or service. It is the essence of who you are as a company and what you stand for in the world of artificial intelligence.

To create a strong brand identity for your AI startup, you must first understand your target audience and what they are looking for in a tech company. Are they seeking innovative solutions to complex problems? Do they value transparency and ethical practices? By defining your target audience and their needs, you can tailor your brand identity to resonate with them on a deeper level.

Once you have a clear understanding of your target audience, it's time to define your brand values and mission statement. What do you want your AI startup to represent in the industry? Are you committed to using AI for social good, or are you focused on helping businesses streamline their operations? Your brand values and mission statement should guide every decision you make as a founder, from product development to marketing strategies.

Next, consider the visual elements of your brand identity, such as your logo, color scheme, and typography. These visual elements should be consistent across all marketing materials and digital platforms to create a cohesive and memorable brand experience for your customers. A strong visual identity will help your AI startup stand out in a crowded market and make a lasting impression on potential clients.

In conclusion, defining your AI startup's brand identity is a foundational step in building a successful tech company from scratch. By understanding your target audience, defining your brand values and mission statement, and creating a cohesive visual identity, you can establish a strong and memorable brand presence in the world of artificial intelligence. Remember, your brand identity is not just a logo or color scheme – it is the essence of who you are as a company and what you stand for in the ever-evolving tech industry.

Marketing Your AI Startup

Marketing your AI startup is a crucial step in building a successful tech company from scratch. As a founder in the ever-evolving world of artificial intelligence, it is essential to understand the unique challenges and opportunities that come with promoting your innovative products and services. With the right strategies and mindset, you can effectively reach your target audience and showcase the value of your AI solutions.

One of the first steps in marketing your AI startup is to clearly define your target market. Understanding the needs and pain points of your potential customers will help you tailor your messaging and positioning to resonate with them. By conducting thorough market research and gathering insights from your target audience, you can create a compelling value proposition that differentiates your AI startup from competitors.

Once you have a deep understanding of your target market, it is important to develop a comprehensive marketing plan that outlines your goals, strategies, and tactics. This plan should include a mix of online and offline marketing channels, such as social media, content marketing, SEO, and paid advertising. By leveraging a combination of digital and traditional marketing techniques, you can maximize your reach and engage with potential customers across different touchpoints.

In addition to traditional marketing tactics, founders of AI startups should also consider leveraging partnerships and collaborations to expand their reach and credibility in the industry. By forming strategic alliances with other tech companies, universities, research institutions, and industry associations, you can tap into new networks and access valuable resources that can help accelerate the growth of your AI startup.

Ultimately, marketing your AI startup is about telling a compelling story that resonates with your target audience and showcases the unique value proposition of your products and services. By staying true to your vision and values, and consistently communicating the benefits of your AI solutions, you can build a strong brand presence and attract loyal customers who believe in the power of artificial intelligence to transform their businesses and lives. Remember, marketing is not just about selling products - it's about building relationships and creating lasting impact in the world of technology and innovation.

Building Partnerships and Alliances

Building partnerships and alliances is crucial for the success of any AI startup. As a Founder in the tech industry, it is important to recognize the power of collaboration in driving innovation and growth. By forming strategic partnerships with other companies, startups, or research institutions, you can leverage their expertise, resources, and networks to propel your own business forward.

One of the key benefits of building partnerships and alliances is the ability to access new markets and customer segments. By aligning yourself with established players in the industry, you can tap into their existing customer base and expand your reach far beyond what would be possible on your own. This can be especially valuable for AI startups looking to scale quickly and establish a strong presence in the market.

In addition to expanding your reach, partnerships can also help you stay at the forefront of technological advancements. By collaborating with other companies that are leaders in their respective fields, you can gain access to cutting-edge technologies, tools, and insights that can give you a competitive edge. This can be particularly beneficial for AI startups, as the field is constantly evolving and staying ahead of the curve is essential for success.

Furthermore, partnerships and alliances can provide valuable learning opportunities for founders. By working closely with other companies, startups, or research institutions, you can exchange knowledge, ideas, and best practices that can help you improve your own processes and strategies. This collaborative approach to business can foster a culture of innovation and continuous improvement within your startup.

In conclusion, building partnerships and alliances is a key strategy for founders looking to create a successful AI startup. By collaborating with other companies, startups, or research institutions, you can access new markets, stay at the forefront of technological advancements, and gain valuable learning opportunities. Embrace the power of collaboration and watch your startup thrive in the competitive world of AI technology.

Chapter 10: Overcoming Challenges and Failures

Dealing with Failure in Your AI Startup

Failure is an inevitable part of the entrepreneurial journey, especially when it comes to building a tech startup in the complex and ever-evolving field of artificial intelligence. As a founder of an AI startup, it is crucial to understand that setbacks and failures are not the end of the road, but rather valuable learning experiences that can propel your business forward. Embracing failure as a stepping stone to success is essential in navigating the challenges that come with building a successful AI startup.

When faced with failure in your AI startup, it is important to maintain a positive and resilient mindset. Recognize that failure is a natural part of the growth process and an opportunity to course-correct and improve. By viewing failure as a learning opportunity, you can extract valuable insights that can help you refine your business strategy, product offerings, and customer experience. Remember, every successful entrepreneur has faced failure at some point in their journey – it is how you respond to these challenges that will ultimately determine your success.

One of the key ways to deal with failure in your AI startup is to seek feedback from mentors, advisors, and industry experts. Surround yourself with a strong support network that can provide guidance, insights, and encouragement during difficult times. Learning from the experiences of others who have successfully navigated failure can help you gain perspective and identify new strategies for overcoming obstacles in your own business. Remember, you are not alone in facing challenges – there are resources and individuals who are willing to support you on your entrepreneurial journey.

In the face of failure, it is important to stay focused on your long-term vision and goals for your AI startup. While setbacks may be discouraging in the short term, maintaining a clear sense of purpose and direction will help you stay motivated and determined to overcome obstacles. Reflect on your initial reasons for starting your AI startup and remind yourself of the impact you aspire to make in the world. By staying true to your mission and values, you can harness the resilience and determination needed to push through failure and achieve success.

Ultimately, failure is not a reflection of your worth as an entrepreneur, but rather a necessary step in the growth and evolution of your AI startup. Embrace failure as a learning opportunity, seek feedback and support from others, and stay focused on your long-term vision. By adopting a positive and resilient mindset, you can turn setbacks into stepping stones towards success and build a thriving AI startup that makes a meaningful impact in the world. Remember, the journey of entrepreneurship is filled with challenges, but it is through overcoming failure that we truly grow and succeed.

Learning from Mistakes and Moving Forward

Mistakes are a natural part of the journey when it comes to building a tech startup, especially in the world of artificial intelligence. As a Founder in the AI space, it is crucial to learn from these mistakes and use them as stepping stones towards future success. Embracing failure as a learning opportunity can lead to valuable insights and growth for both yourself and your company.

One of the key lessons to take away from mistakes is the importance of resilience. Building an AI startup from scratch is no easy feat, and setbacks are bound to happen along the way. It is essential to have the resilience to bounce back from these setbacks, learn from them, and keep moving forward. Remember, every mistake is a chance to grow stronger and more resilient as a Founder.

Another valuable lesson to learn from mistakes is the power of adaptation. In the fast-paced world of AI technology, being able to adapt quickly to changing circumstances is crucial for success. Mistakes can often highlight areas where your startup needs to adapt and evolve. Use these insights to pivot your strategy, refine your approach, and stay ahead of the curve in the competitive AI market.

Furthermore, mistakes can also provide valuable insights into the strengths and weaknesses of your team. As a Founder, it is important to foster a culture of openness and transparency within your team. Encourage team members to share their mistakes and learn from each other's experiences. By collectively learning from mistakes, your team can become stronger, more cohesive, and better equipped to tackle the challenges of building an AI startup.

In conclusion, learning from mistakes is a crucial part of the journey as a Founder in the AI space. Embrace failure as a learning opportunity, cultivate resilience, adapt quickly, and foster a culture of openness within your team. By applying these principles, you can turn mistakes into valuable lessons that propel your AI startup towards success. Remember, it's not about how many mistakes you make, but how you learn from them and keep moving forward.

Staying Resilient and Persistent in Building Your AI Startup

As a founder of an AI startup, it is important to stay resilient and persistent in the face of challenges. Building a tech startup from scratch is no easy feat, especially in the rapidly evolving world of artificial intelligence. However, with dedication and perseverance, you can overcome obstacles and achieve success.

One of the key traits of successful founders is their ability to bounce back from setbacks and keep moving forward. It is important to remember that failure is not the end, but rather an opportunity to learn and grow. By staying resilient in the face of adversity, you can turn obstacles into stepping stones towards your ultimate goal of building a successful AI startup.

Persistence is another crucial quality that all founders must possess. Building a tech startup requires a lot of hard work and dedication, and it is easy to become discouraged when things don't go as planned. However, by staying persistent and continuing to push forward, you can overcome any challenges that come your way.

In the world of AI startups, innovation is key. By staying resilient and persistent, you can continue to push the boundaries of what is possible in the field of artificial intelligence. Don't be afraid to think outside the box and try new approaches - it is often through failure that we discover new and innovative solutions.

In conclusion, building an AI startup requires a combination of resilience and persistence. By staying true to your vision and never giving up, you can overcome any obstacles that come your way and achieve success. Remember, the road to building a successful tech startup may be tough, but with determination and perseverance, you can make your dreams a reality.

Chapter 11: The Future of AI Startups

Trends and Innovations in the AI Industry

In today's fast-paced technological landscape, staying ahead of the curve is crucial for any founder looking to break into the AI industry. The trends and innovations shaping the AI industry are constantly evolving, presenting both challenges and opportunities for those bold enough to innovate. As a founder, it is essential to keep a pulse on the latest advancements in AI to ensure your startup remains competitive and relevant in the market.

One of the most significant trends in the AI industry is the rise of explainable AI. As AI systems become increasingly complex and powerful, understanding how they arrive at their decisions is becoming more critical. Explainable AI aims to demystify the black box nature of AI algorithms, providing transparency and accountability. By incorporating explainable AI into your startup's offerings, you can build trust with customers and regulators, setting yourself apart from the competition.

Another exciting trend in the AI industry is the convergence of AI and other cutting-edge technologies, such as blockchain and quantum computing. These interdisciplinary collaborations are pushing the boundaries of what is possible with AI, opening up new avenues for innovation and disruption. By exploring these intersections and embracing a multidisciplinary approach, you can unlock new opportunities for your AI startup and differentiate yourself in the market.

Innovations in natural language processing (NLP) and computer vision are also reshaping the AI industry, enabling more personalized and intuitive interactions between humans and machines. By leveraging these advancements in your AI startup, you can create more engaging and user-friendly products and services that resonate with your target audience. Whether it's developing chatbots that can understand natural language or implementing image recognition technology for enhanced customer experiences, the possibilities are endless with NLP and computer vision.

As a founder in the AI industry, it is crucial to embrace these trends and innovations with an open mind and a willingness to experiment. By staying nimble and adaptable, you can position your startup for success in an ever-evolving landscape. Remember, the key to building a thriving AI startup lies in your ability to anticipate trends, harness innovations, and pivot when necessary. With a pioneering spirit and a commitment to continuous learning, you can chart a course for your AI startup's success and make a lasting impact in the industry.

Adapting to Technological Advances in AI

In today's fast-paced world, technological advances in artificial intelligence are revolutionizing the way we do business. As a founder looking to create an AI startup, it is crucial to adapt to these changes and stay ahead of the curve. By embracing new technologies and incorporating them into your business model, you can position yourself as a leader in the industry and drive innovation in ways you never thought possible.

One of the key ways to adapt to technological advances in AI is to invest in ongoing education and training for yourself and your team. By staying up-to-date on the latest developments in AI, you can ensure that your startup is always at the forefront of innovation. This may involve attending workshops, conferences, or enrolling in online courses to deepen your understanding of AI and how it can be applied to your business.

Another important aspect of adapting to technological advances in AI is to foster a culture of experimentation and risk-taking within your startup. By encouraging your team to think outside the box and try new approaches, you can unlock the full potential of AI and discover innovative solutions to complex challenges. Embrace failure as a learning opportunity and use it to fuel your growth and development as a company.

Furthermore, it is essential to collaborate with other industry leaders and experts in the field of AI to exchange ideas, share best practices, and stay informed about emerging trends. By building a strong network of professionals in the AI space, you can tap into a wealth of knowledge and expertise that can help propel your startup to new heights. Surround yourself with like-minded individuals who are passionate about AI and are committed to pushing the boundaries of what is possible.

In conclusion, adapting to technological advances in AI is essential for any founder looking to create a successful AI startup. By embracing new technologies, investing in education and training, fostering a culture of experimentation, and collaborating with industry leaders, you can position your startup as a trailblazer in the world of AI. Stay inspired, stay innovative, and never stop pushing the boundaries of what is possible with artificial intelligence.

Continuing to Innovate and Disrupt in the AI Market

As a Founder in the competitive world of AI startups, it is crucial to always stay ahead of the curve by continuing to innovate and disrupt in the market. The AI landscape is constantly evolving, with new technologies and trends emerging at a rapid pace. To succeed in this fast-paced environment, it is essential to embrace change and push the boundaries of what is possible with artificial intelligence.

One way to stay ahead in the AI market is to foster a culture of innovation within your startup. Encourage your team to think outside the box and experiment with new ideas and technologies. By fostering a culture of innovation, you can create a dynamic and forward-thinking company that is always at the forefront of the latest AI trends.

In addition to fostering a culture of innovation, it is also important to disrupt the market with groundbreaking products and services. Look for ways to challenge the status quo and offer unique solutions to complex problems. By disrupting the market, you can differentiate your startup from the competition and attract a loyal customer base that is eager to embrace cutting-edge AI technologies.

Furthermore, it is essential to stay informed about the latest trends and developments in the AI market. Attend industry conferences, participate in networking events, and engage with thought leaders in the field. By staying informed, you can gain valuable insights into emerging trends and technologies, and position your startup as a leader in the AI market.

In conclusion, as a Founder in the AI market, it is crucial to continue to innovate and disrupt in order to stay ahead of the competition. By fostering a culture of innovation, disrupting the market with groundbreaking products and services, and staying informed about the latest trends, you can position your startup for success in the ever-evolving world of artificial intelligence. Embrace change, push the boundaries of what is possible, and continue to strive for excellence in all that you do.

Chapter 12: Conclusion

Reflecting on Your Journey as an AI Startup Founder

As a founder of an AI startup, it is important to take the time to reflect on your journey and the progress you have made so far. Building a tech startup from scratch is no easy feat, and as an AI founder, you have embarked on a challenging and exciting adventure. Reflecting on your journey allows you to take stock of your accomplishments, learn from your failures, and set new goals for the future.

Think back to the moment when you first had the idea for your AI startup. Perhaps you were struck by a problem that could be solved with the power of artificial intelligence, or maybe you saw an opportunity in the market that no one else had yet capitalized on. Whatever the spark that ignited your journey, it is important to remember that your vision and determination have brought you to where you are today.

Consider the challenges you have faced along the way. From securing funding to building a talented team, launching a successful AI startup requires overcoming numerous obstacles. Reflect on how you have navigated these challenges with resilience and creativity. Your ability to adapt and innovate in the face of adversity is what sets you apart as an AI founder.

Celebrate your successes, both big and small. Whether you have secured your first major client, launched a groundbreaking product, or received recognition in the industry, take the time to acknowledge and appreciate your achievements. Remember that every milestone reached is a testament to your hard work and dedication as an AI startup founder.

Looking ahead, set new goals and aspirations for your AI startup. Reflect on where you want to take your company in the future and what steps you need to take to get there. Remember that the journey of building a tech startup is a continuous process of growth and evolution. Stay inspired, stay focused, and continue to push the boundaries of what is possible in the world of AI entrepreneurship.

Celebrating Your Successes and Milestones

As a founder of an AI startup, it's essential to take the time to celebrate your successes and milestones along the way. Building a tech startup from scratch is no easy feat, and it's important to acknowledge the hard work and dedication that has gotten you to where you are today. By celebrating your successes, you not only boost morale and motivation within your team but also inspire others in the industry to strive for greatness.

Each milestone reached in your AI startup journey is a testament to your vision and determination. Whether it's securing your first round of funding, launching a successful product, or landing a key partnership, these achievements deserve to be recognized and celebrated. Take the time to reflect on how far you've come and the obstacles you've overcome to get to this point. Remember that each success, no matter how small, is a step closer to achieving your ultimate goals.

Celebrating your successes and milestones is not just about throwing a party or patting yourself on the back. It's about acknowledging the hard work, dedication, and perseverance that has gone into building your AI startup. By recognizing and celebrating your achievements, you reinforce a culture of positivity and success within your team. This positive energy can propel your startup to even greater heights and inspire others in the industry to push themselves to new limits.

In the fast-paced world of tech startups, it's easy to get caught up in the day-to-day grind and forget to celebrate the wins along the way. However, taking the time to acknowledge and celebrate your successes is crucial for maintaining motivation and momentum in your AI startup. By celebrating your milestones, you remind yourself and your team of the progress you've made and the potential for even greater success in the future.

So, as you navigate the challenging and exciting world of building an AI startup, remember to take the time to celebrate your successes and milestones. Whether it's a small victory or a major achievement, each step forward is worth recognizing and celebrating. By acknowledging your successes, you not only inspire yourself and your team but also set the stage for even greater accomplishments in the future. Keep pushing forward, stay positive, and never underestimate the power of celebrating your successes along the way.

Looking Ahead to the Future of Your AI Startup

As a founder, it's important to always be looking ahead to the future of your AI startup. The technology landscape is constantly evolving, and it's crucial to stay ahead of the curve in order to remain competitive in the market. In this subchapter, we will explore some key strategies for ensuring the long-term success of your AI startup.

One of the most important things to keep in mind when looking ahead to the future of your AI startup is the need to constantly innovate. The field of artificial intelligence is rapidly advancing, and it's essential to stay on top of the latest trends and developments in order to remain relevant. By investing in research and development and staying abreast of industry news, you can ensure that your startup is always at the cutting edge of technology.

Another key aspect of planning for the future of your AI startup is to focus on building a strong team. Surrounding yourself with talented and dedicated individuals who share your vision for the company is essential for long-term success. By hiring the right people and fostering a culture of collaboration and innovation, you can create a team that is capable of taking your startup to new heights.

It's also important to think about scalability when looking ahead to the future of your AI startup. As your company grows, you will need to be able to scale your operations in order to meet the increasing demand for your products and services. By planning for growth from the outset and investing in scalable infrastructure, you can ensure that your startup is well-positioned for success in the long term.

In conclusion, the future of your AI startup is in your hands. By staying ahead of the curve, fostering a culture of innovation, building a strong team, and planning for scalability, you can ensure that your company is well-positioned for success in the years to come. Keep pushing the boundaries of what is possible with artificial intelligence, and you will be well on your way to building a tech startup that is truly revolutionary.